SCRIPTURES IN POETRY

By Beverley Phipps

ASPECT Books
www.ASPECTBooks.com

World rights reserved. This book or any portion thereof may not be copied or reproduced in any form or manner whatever, except as provided by law, without the written permission of the publisher, except by a reviewer who may quote brief passages in a review.

The author assumes full responsibility for the accuracy of all facts and quotations as cited in this book. The opinions expressed in this book are the author's personal views and interpretations, and do not necessarily reflect those of the publisher.

This book is provided with the understanding that the publisher is not engaged in giving spiritual, legal, medical, or other professional advice. If authoritative advice is needed, the reader should seek the counsel of a competent professional.

Copyright © 2024 Beverley Phipps

Copyright © 2024 ASPECT Books

ISBN-13: 978-1-4796-1795-1 (Paperback)

Library of Congress Control Number: 2024907923

Published by

ASPECT Books
www.ASPECTBooks.com

Table of Contents

THE GREAT CONTROVERSY 7

ADAM AND EVE 8

NOAH 9

ABRAHAM 10

SODOM AND GOMORRAH 11

JOSEPH 12

MOSES 13

SAMSON'S FOLLY 14

SAUL 15

DAVID 16

SOLOMON 17

ELIJAH 18

ELISHA 18

JOB 19

ISAIAH 20

JEREMIAH 20

DANIEL 21

JONAH 22

LAW 23

    THE SABBATH 23

    HONOR YOUR PARENTS 24

    TAKING A LIFE 24

    GOD'S PRECIOUS GIFT 25

- HIGHER STANDARDS ... 25
  - LYING ... 26
  - ENVY ... 26
- MARY AND JOSEPH ... 27
- THE PASSOVER ... 27
- CHRIST'S BAPTISM ... 28
- THE TEMPTATION ... 28
- THE MARRIAGE AT CANA ... 29
- THE SYRO-PHOENICIAN WOMAN ... 29
- THE BLIND BEGGAR ... 30
- FEEDING THE FIVE THOUSAND ... 30
- THE MAN BORN BLIND ... 31
- THE POOL OF BETHESDA ... 31
- WALKING ON THE WATER ... 32
- JESUS RAISES LAZARUS ... 32
- THE WIDOW OF NAIN ... 33
- THE TEN LEPERS ... 33
- THE WILD MAN ... 33
- THE MAN WITH PALSY ... 34
- JAIRUS' DAUGHTER & THE ISSUE OF BLOOD ... 35
- TWO BLIND MEN ... 35
- THE STORM ... 36
- THE WITHERED HAND ... 36
- THE BLIND AND SPEECHLESS MAN ... 36
- THE CENTURION'S SERVANT ... 37

THE BEATITUDES	37
THE LIFE OF CHRIST	38
THE SACRIFICIAL LAMB	38
THE PASSOVER FEAST	39
GETHSEMANE	40
CAIAPHAS	41
PILATE'S JUDGMENT HALL	42
THE CROSS	43
RESURRECTION MORNING	43
WORTH IT ALL	44
JESUS	44
THE PRODIGAL SON	45
THE PHARISEE AND PUBLICAN	45
THE GOOD SAMARITAN	46
THE VINEYARD	46
THE WHEAT AND THE TARES	47
THE TALENTS	47
THE LABORERS	48
THE TREASURES	48
THE SOWER	49
THE ROYAL FEAST	49
THE RICH MAN WITH PLENTY	50
THE LOST SHEEP	50
THE WEDDING FEAST	51
THE TWO HOUSES	51

THE TEN VIRGINS	52
THE LOST COIN	52
POWER	53
FOOD FROM HEAVEN	54
PETER'S VISION	55
PETER'S ESCAPE	56
DORCAS	56
STEPHEN	57
THE ROAD TO DAMASCUS	58
JUPITER AND MERCURY	59
MACEDONIA	60
MARS HILL	61
PAUL'S WORK IN CORINTH	62
PAUL'S YEARS IN EPHESUS	62
PAUL'S LENGTHY SERMON	63
DANGER IN JERUSALEM	64
DANGER IN JERUSALEM (cont.)	65
SHIPWRECKED	66
MELITA	67

THE GREAT CONTROVERSY

One day in the courts of heaven Lucifer began to doubt.
Questioned God's eternal precepts, Jesus had to throw him out.
"No way will I stand in silence. Man will fall because of me,"
Satan boasted to his angels, who left heaven, tearfully.
Man, of course, became the victim of this cunning, wily foe.
Christ is pleading, gently pleading, "Please come home. I love you so."
Jesus says, "I love you dearly. Follow Me and you shall live.
Even though you caused Me sorrow, all your sins I will forgive."
Satan says, "What's love? That's crazy! Follow me and laugh and live.
I can't offer life unending, but I'll make it lucrative."
Jesus says, "I love you dearly. Follow Me and you shall live.
I will pardon all transgressions if your all you'll freely give."
Satan says, "What's love? That's crazy! Follow me and laugh and live.
You'll have fun, though death awaits you. I have nothing more to give."
Life and death are put before us. We must choose which way to go.
Christ will win this controversy. Sin and death He'll overthrow.

ADAM AND EVE

When God stooped down upon the ground and formed a lump of clay,
He breathed in him the breath of life. A soul was made that day.
When Adam saw the animals look on their mates with pride,
He said aloud, "I need someone to be here by my side."
So God caused him to go to sleep and opened Adam's chest.
He took a rib out of his side and made the very best.
And now, he had a soul mate who was custom made for him—
So beautiful to look upon, so warm, so feminine.
And God said, "Do not separate. Stay near you lovely bride."
But somehow, Eve just drifted off, and left her husband's side.
Now, slightly hidden in a tree where they were not to go,
There, coiled among the branches was this cunning, wily foe.
"Please come a little closer, dear and eat this fruit, so fair."
"O no, we cannot touch that fruit. To eat it I don't dare".
"This fruit is good. I'm eating it," The devil said to Eve.
"Jehovah is afraid because Nirvana you'll achieve."
It really looked inviting, so, she took a little bite,
And right away she felt herself ascend to greater heights.
She ran to Adam in her bliss. "Here, eat this fruit with me."
"O, Eve, what have you done, my Dear? You acted foolishly."
Then Adam also ate the fruit—He feared he'd lose his wife.
Because they disobeyed their Lord, this world is full of strife.
But God devised a plan to save mankind from every sin.
Christ shed His blood to rescue us and bring us back to Him.

NOAH

One day, Mr. Noah said, "I think I'll build a boat.
God told me He'll send a flood, and we must stay afloat."
Never had it rained before. They thought he'd lost his mind.
He said, "Water's going to come and wipe out all mankind."
People came from far and near to laugh, to stare and gawk.
For one hundred twenty years he listened to them mock.
When the boat was done, at last, God called His creatures in,
Every species in the world, and every specimen.
Noah and his family then, went in that crude shaped boat.
Eight of them were safe and sound where they could stay afloat.
God then shut the vessel's door, and for about a week,
Not a raindrop was in sight. They thought he was a freak.
People came from all around to poke a lot of fun.
Crazy Noah in a boat, when there was all that sun!
When they laughed 'til they were hoarse, all people large and small,
Thunder pealed across the sky and rain began to fall.
Then they pounded on the door. "Old Noah, let us in.
We will gladly do what's right. We now confess our sin."
God's the One who shut the door. Their pleas were made too late.
Water swallowed them alive, each sinful reprobate.
Only Noah and his wife and family were inside.
When God's mercy closed that day, their lives were justified.
There's another door that God is going to close, my friend.
Mercy's door is open, now. Oh, won't you enter in?
When He stands and says, "It's done. Your destiny is sealed."
Will it be too late for you? Please heed His last appeal.
God is calling you today to give your life to Him.
Don't be shut outside the door and never enter in.

ABRAHAM

Mr. Terah had a son. He named him Abraham.
God said, "Get thee from your land. Take all your herds and clan."
Then God said, "Look way up high, see all the starry sights.
I will multiply your seed and match them with those lights."
Abraham lost all his faith; depended on himself.
Hagar bore a son for him. They called him Ishmael.
God said, "No, he's not the one. Your wife, a son will bear.
When he's born into your home, he'll be the promised heir."
Isaac came into his life and joy was everywhere.
Sarah treated this dear son with love and tender care.
Sarah heard this other son make fun of Isaac, so,
She told Abraham, right then, "These people have to go."
Traveling in the wilderness, their water soon was gone.
Hagar left poor Ishmael to die beneath the sun.
God came down and rescued them. She found a well nearby.
Precious water! What a treat! She knew they would not die.
Abraham talked with his God. Communion was serene.
Family life was quite ideal. God's law was held supreme.
"Abraham, it's time to go," God said, when day was done.
"Sacrifice this tender youth. I want your only son."
Abraham obeyed God's call, took Isaac to the mount,
Raised the knife into the air. This was a sad account.
Just before he plunged the knife to slay this precious lad,
God said, "No! I've seen enough." And both of them were glad.
In the thicket was a ram he found to use instead.
Isaac sat up thankfully—came down from his deathbed.
Abraham, this faithful soul, lay down and closed his eyes,
Waiting for his Lord to come, to be in Paradise.

SODOM AND GOMORRAH

Sodom and Gomorrah were two very evil towns.
Wickedness was everywhere. Corruption did abound.
Lot decided he would go and pitch his tent nearby.
Never dreaming he would leave and say his last goodbye.
Two men came to visit him. The men nearby exclaimed,
"Let's make sport with these two guys, and play our little game."
"No," said Lot, "I have some girls. Please play your game with them."
Those were angels in his home. They blinded those warped men.
Then the angels said to him, "We'll burn these cities down.
Take your wife and family, and flee. Get out of town.
Don't look back or turn around. Don't hesitate or halt."
Mrs. Lot did not obey. Her body turned to salt.
God rained fire from above and burned those cities down.
Every lofty edifice was burned right to the ground.
Lot got drunk. His daughters, then, devised a wicked game.
He became the father of their children. What a shame.
It is never safe to play with fire in your soul.
Give yourself to Jesus; He will surely make you whole.
Don't stay close to evil. It will be your great demise.
Lift your thoughts to heaven, or your soul you'll jeopardize.

JOSEPH

A man named Jacob had a favorite son. A little self-centered, I'd say.
He dreamed his brothers would bow down to him.
They scoffed at what he had to say.
When Jacob made his son a pretty coat, so colorful, like the rainbow,
The brothers hated what their father did. Quite frequently they told him so.
His brothers left to go feed all the flock. I guess when they tarried too long,
Old Jacob worried and called for his son to find them and see what went wrong.
Now, Joseph, being eager to obey, was happy as he took his stroll.
He wanted desperately to show that he was daring, courageous and bold.
And Joseph found them and all their flock in Dothan, out there on the range.
"Let's kill this fellow who has all the dreams."
Their thoughts and ideas were deranged.
But Reuben whispered, "We cannot do that.
Let's put him down deep in this pit."
When Reuben left to do some other things, they sold him, they had to admit.
They took the coat that they had dipped in blood, presented it to their old Dad.
And Jacob cried as though his heart would break,
because of the grief that he had.
In Egypt, Potiphar would hire him. He put all he had in his hand.
But Mrs. Potiphar was evil when she tried to seduce that young man.
And when he turned around to leave her side, she held on to Joseph's coattail.
Of course, when Potiphar was told this thing,
poor Joseph was marched off to jail.
One day he managed to get out of jail by telling old Pharaoh his dream.
So he was put in charge of all the land, to oversee was his routine.
For seven years he stored the corn and grain,
and when the lean years had begun,
Because of Joseph and his expertise, nobody went hungry, not one.
In Canaan, Jacob had run out of food. His sons had to travel quite far.
They went to Egypt, and you know the rest. They met with a tale quite bizarre.
But when it ended, Jacob found his son and moved into Egypt to stay.
The brothers settled all their differences, and everything turned out okay.

MOSES

Moses' mother made a boat, put slime and pitch around it;
Floated him upon the Nile, and Pharaoh's daughter found it.
When the baby cried aloud, her heart was filled with pity.
"Take this baby home for me. He's precious and so pretty."
Safe within the palace walls, he grew and prospered well,
Guided by the principles his mother did instill.
When he killed an overseer, old Pharaoh sought to slay him.
Moses fled to Midian because of all the mayhem.
One day out in Jethro's field he saw a bush on fire;
Had to take his sandals off before he could inquire.
God said, "Set My people free. I'll help you in your mission.
I'll prepare the way for you and bring it to fruition."
God sent many plagues to them, but Pharaoh's heart was hardened.
He refused to let them go. The Hebrews were disheartened.
Plagues of lice, and flies and frogs, and boils and hail and locusts.
Finally his son was dead, and Pharaoh lost his focus.
"Get you out! Be gone before I tear your face asunder!"
Moses led them through the sea, but Pharaoh's host went under.
God called Moses to the mount where conduct rules were spoken.
"Everything You say, we'll do, but promises were broken.
They complained about the food, and then about the water.
Moses went into a rage. His blood kept getting hotter.
Struck the rock when God said, speak. His wandering days were over.
Went upon the mountain top, was buried 'neath the clover.
What a punishment this was for one who disobeyed Him.
Moses thought that all was lost, his heart was heavy-laden.
God did not forsake His friend, there's yet a happy ending.
Now he walks on streets of gold and has a life unending.

SAMSON'S FOLLY

Mrs. Manoah had a son. Her heart was filled with song.
As he grew up, became a man, she let his hair grow long.
Samson's great strength, his might and power were found in his long hair.
"Don't put a razor on his head," the angel did declare.
"Take no wine, nor unclean thing," the angel cautioned her.
"I want this child to grow up strong," he told her earlier.
Samson grew up and reached the age when hormones multiply.
He saw this lovely Philistine. Her beauty caught his eye.
"Get her for me. I want her now," he told his mom and dad.
"Why can't you find one in the church? You make our hearts quite sad."
"Get her for me. I want her now," was all that he would say.
Just to keep peace, they coddled him and said it was OK.
After he slew a lion, bold, and haggled for his life,
Samson slew thirty Philistines, but lost his pretty wife.
When his good friend had married her, he found some foxes near.
Tying their tails with firebrands, his heart began to cheer.
After he set their tails on fire, he put them in the field,
Burning their crops down to the ground. The sight was quite unreal.
And then he met Miss Delilah—so warm, so soft, so fair.
She was so gorgeous to look upon, with long and flowing hair.
She tricked him to tell the secret of why he was so strong.
Somebody cut off his tresses, while sleeping in her arms.
They bound him with some heavy ropes, and gouged out both his eyes.
He was blind the rest of his life until he met his demise.
When Samson asked God for pardon, his hair began to grow.
He killed more of the Philistines than you will ever know.
And when he pulled the Temple down that killed them one and all,
He lost his life in the rubble when bricks began to fall.
Because he truly repented, eternal life he'll gain,
He'll have a place up in heaven when Jesus comes to reign.

SAUL

Now, in the days of Samuel, the Lord God, Himself, ruled supreme.
But were the people satisfied? Oh, no! They just wanted a king.
So Samuel went to God in prayer. God said, "I will do as they say.
Go look for someone to be king, and maybe they'll learn to obey."
Now, in the tribe of Benjamin, there was a male offspring named Kish.
His son was handsome, tall and fair. So how could the people resist?
And Saul was made the ruling king. Son, Jonathan, was his delight.
At times Saul's problems conquered him. He just couldn't sleep in the night.
Then David came to play his harp to soothe all his trouble away.
One night the crazed and troubled Saul tried hard to put David away.
Because his son liked David so, he tried to kill Jonathan, too.
He threw a spear at that poor boy, but Jon moved and quickly withdrew.
Saul hated David 'til he died, but David respected his king.
He hounded him relentlessly, though David had not done a thing.
Saul went into a cave one day to cover his feet, so they say.
And David cut Saul's royal robe to prove he could blow him away.
Saul seemed to lose his intellect. His actions were not always wise.
Instead of seeking out his God, he went to a witch for advice.
Saul asked to see old Samuel, who died and was buried before.
Instead, up came a phantom ghost, who told him he'd die in the war.
Saul always fought the Philistines. They usually caused trouble for him.
He seemed to always be ahead, though sometimes his chances were slim.
The Philistines prevailed at last, and Saul's sons were killed in the fray.
They also wounded Saul, the king, who took his own life on that day.
Saul died because of his great sin, in seeking a witch for advice.
When Saul let Satan be his god, he transgressed and met his demise.

DAVID

There was a young shepherd named David, the youngest of Jesse, we're told.
While tending the sheep of his father, he pulled off some things that were bold.
He met with a bear and a lion; they picked up a poor little lamb.
He walked up to them without flinching, and tore at them with his bare hands.
So when he encountered a giant, he wasn't afraid to take aim.
He picked up some stones and a sling shot
and brought down that oversized frame.
His music was smooth and majestic. He knew how to play and to sing.
A prophet named Samuel ordained him to take on new duties as king.
One day he walked out on his terrace—
saw something that made his eyes bulge.
Bathsheba, in all of her beauty was bathing. He had to indulge.
And when he found out she was fruitful, he murdered the man in his way.
He ended up sending Uriah to die in the battle that day.
But God sent a prophet named Nathan to show David where he went wrong.
His sorrow was real. He repented, and wrote many heart-rending songs.
To show he was sorry for sinning, he wanted a house for his Lord.
But God said, "There's blood on your fingers." So Solomon finished the chore.
Though David had riches and glory, rebellion was spread far and wide.
His son, Absalom, undermined him, and David shed tears when he died.
Despite all his sins and shortcomings, God held him in highest regard.
He labeled this sorry transgressor, a man with a heart like his Lord.

SOLOMON

Solomon asked God to give him wisdom from above.
He wrote many proverbs, showed God's mercy and His love.
Solomon, the wisest man this world has ever seen,
Let his riches get to him and did things to extreme.
Solomon had many wives and mistresses galore.
And the Queen of Sheba came to knock upon his door.
Solomon, the wisest man, held in such great esteem,
Soon became the biggest fool this world has ever seen.
Threw away the wisdom that the Lord bestowed on him,
Took his moral principles and tossed them to the wind.
When he realized that all was vanity and more,
He repented of his sins and served God as before.
After he had done his thing and turned his life around,
He wrote words of wisdom that were morally profound.
Forty years this sovereign king ruled in Jerusalem.
When he died they buried him right there in Bethlehem.

ELIJAH

Elijah was a man of God. Not many wanted to hear
The messages he brought to them. They laughed and wanted to jeer.
For they were Baal worshipers, the god that Jezebel knew.
To them, he was the only god, the best, in their point of view.
It had not rained for quite some time. Of course, Elijah was blamed.
He put old Ahab to the test to see whose God would send rain.
"Let's all go to the mountain top and pray for water to fall.
Whichever God sends fire down will be the God of us all."
They cried aloud for Baal to hear. He never uttered a peep.
Elijah then cried out to them, "Perhaps your god is asleep.
Or maybe Baal went on a trip. He might have gone out of town."
The people cut themselves with knives 'til blood gushed out on the ground.
And when it was Elijah's turn to pray and ask God for rain,
He poured a lot of water on the altar, and in the drain.
At last, the Lord sent fire down. The sacrifice was consumed.
It burned the altar, wood and stones, and all the water and fumes.
The rain came down in torrents, too. God's name was then glorified.
And Jezebel then sought revenge. Elijah ran off to hide.
An angel took good care of him, and gave him food he could eat.
And Jezebel could do no harm. God gave Elijah a treat.
He sent a fiery chariot down to swoop him up in the sky.
This faithful servant of the Lord now reigns with Jesus on high.

ELISHA

Elisha, the prophet, was strolling along a rough pathway one day.
Mean-spirited fellows approached him, and this is what they had to say,
"Hey, baldy, sprout wings and start flying up yonder like Elijah did."
Some bears, then, came out of the forest, and ate them, right down to their ribs.
Another time when he went strolling, he traveled a long time one day.
He was so hungry and famished he stopped for a moment to pray.
And God led him to a poor widow who started to bake her last bread
To give to her son, who was hungry, then, he could no longer be fed.
"First, let me partake of your morsel. I promise your son will not die.
Let me eat before you are nourished, and all your needs God will supply."
Because she was kind to Elisha with food she provided for him,
God kept her in flour and oil. They never went hungry again.

JOB

Satan was out to get poor Job, as he realized one day.
Honesty and integrity somehow were brought into play.
God said, "Don't put a hand on him or touch him in any way.
Only the things that he holds dear, I'll let you destroy today."
Satan then set about the task to knock all Job's servants down.
Sabeans were unmerciful while killing them, all but one.
Satan then brought a fire down and killed all his sheep and cows,
Also the servants watching them. One servant escaped, somehow.
Then, some Chaldeans came upon Job's camels and took them all,
Killing the servants as they went, one managing not to fall.
Satan then caused a mighty wind to wipe all Job's family out.
His sons and his daughters all were dead. The winds tossed them all about.
Job, through it all, was true to God, gave praise to His holy name.
Never blamed Him for anything, through all of his grief and pain.
Satan approached God once again, "I'll make Job fall in disgrace.
Put forth Your hand and touch his skin, he'll curse You right to Your face."
"Try him," God said, "he'll stay upright, and put him through pain and strife.
He will not fail Me, come what may. You just cannot take his life."
Job went through misery and pain, with boils from his head to toe.
"Curse God and die," his dear wife said, "and stop all this pain and woe."
Three friends then came to comfort him, but blamed all the curse on him.
Job, with his smelly fetid breath said, "I did not delve in sin."
After awhile, God said, "That's all, you can't touch him anymore.
Job is a faithful, upright man. His happiness I'll restore."
God blessed the latter end of Job more than He did the first.
Gave him more children, cows and sheep, removed Satan's wicked curse.
Job lived to praise God many years, had grandsons that he adored.
Then he lay down and went to sleep, awaiting his coming Lord.

ISAIAH

When Isaiah caught a glimpse of Jesus on His throne,
"Woe is me," he cried aloud, I'm wicked and undone."
He was given visions of the Savior's humble birth,
Saw the devil fall from grace and ousted to this earth.
Saw the coming of the Lord when righteous dead will rise,
And at last, the faithful few will meet Him in the skies.
Babylon, the Great would fall, Isaiah prophesied.
Not a soul would sleep in it, nobody would reside.
Don't go near astrologers. They'll be consumed with fire.
Don't take up with stargazers. They too will soon expire.
All who eat the flesh of swine will be consumed at last.
Even those who eat the mouse will also be outcast.
And he wrote about the time when things will be made new.
We'll plant vineyards, eat the fruit and keep the Sabbath, too.

JEREMIAH

Jeremiah wrote God's covenant with man:
How His law was in the heart. That was God's only plan.
If God's people search for Him and seek Him with their hearts,
They will surely find their Lord. His grace He still imparts.
"If you warn the wicked man," God told EZEKIEL,
"And he turns away from sin, he will not burn in hell.
I will give him a new heart and take away the stone.
He will have a heart of flesh. He'll be my very own."

DANIEL

In the book of Daniel there's a fascinating tale.
Four young men were captured, went to Babylon to dwell.
When they went to dinner they refused the royal meat.
"Give us beans and water. That is what we want to eat."
In the end, when tested, they were healthy, strong and wise.
No one looked more wholesome, much to everyone's surprise.
When the king had dreamed of something that he just forgot,
Daniel and the Hebrew boys sought answers from their God.
Then the king began to think about this head of gold.
He, alone, deserved all praise, was arrogant and bold.
Built this golden image, told all creatures great and small,
When the music sounded, on their knees they had to fall.
Now, these Hebrew children just refused to bow the knee
To a man-made idol. Jesus listened to their plea.
Saved them from the furnace, walked among them while they prayed.
Not a hair was damaged in this fiery escapade.
When Belshazzar feasted, Someone wrote upon the wall.
It was kind of eerie—just a hand began to scrawl.
Daniel told that ruler, "You have reached your Waterloo."
Medes and Persians conquered, chained and killed Belshazzar, too.
When Darius governed, wicked men began to plot.
They knew Daniel always knelt and prayed before his God.
So they tricked Darius, and he signed a death decree.
No one dared to pray to God or offer up a plea.
Now, the king was fretful. Daniel faced an awful tomb.
In the den of lions Daniel went to meet his doom.
All the lions smelled him, but they didn't give a lick.
Daniel lasted through the night. His skin was just too thick.
Daniel dreamed of bears and goats, and beasts you can't define.
But he had to seal his book until the end of time.

JONAH

One evening God spoke to old Jonah, "To Nineveh you must go.
The city is wicked and evil, and I'm going to cut it low."
But Jonah decided to vanish, to hide from the Lord, you see.
He hopped on a boat bound for Tarshish, from God he would surely flee.
But God said, "Now Jonah, you'll travel to Nineveh, as I said.
You'll have to get out of this vessel, go under the boat instead."
So God caused a high wind to bluster. The boat almost fell apart.
And Jonah said, "Please throw me over." (I know that it sounds bizarre.)
When Jonah was thrown from the vessel, God sent him a great big whale,
That opened wide and received him, three days in this little jail.
But Jonah cried out to his Maker, "I'll go where you lead me, Lord.
Release me from this little prison. I surely will preach Your word."
So Jonah went through that big city. The people were changed throughout.
And God spared that city from ruin, but Jonah sat down to pout.
"I cannot believe You would do this! Just kill me so I can die."
He built him a booth to get under, and sat down to pout and to cry.
The sun was quite hot in the heavens. To keep Jonah cool and dry,
God caused a big gourd to develop, and gave him some shade nearby.
But God said, "He still needs a lesson. He needs to depend on Me."
God sent a big worm to devour and wither the gourd, you see.
Now, Jonah was livid and angry, but finally he saw the light.
Because all the people repented, God rescued them from their plight.

LAW

High upon the mountain God spoke His holy law.
When the thunder sounded, His people stood in awe.
Have no gods before Me, don't even bow the knee.
Speak My name in reverence. You're Mine exclusively.
Keep My Sabbaths holy, respect your parents, too.
You won't slay your neighbor. Adultery is taboo.
You won't steal or pilfer. You will not speak a lie.
Don't be filled with envy, nor want your neighbor's bride.
When these words were spoken, a covenant was vowed.
You will be My people, and I will be your God.

Remember the Sabbath day to keep it holy....
The seventh day is the Sabbath of the Lord your God.

THE SABBATH

God gave to us the Sabbath day to rest from every care.
He set aside a sacred time where He could meet us there.
Each precious, sacred moment is reserved for God above.
We put aside our earthly cares and revel in His love.
God blessed a little part of time cut from eternity.
He gave the Sabbath day to man and said, "Remember Me."
There never would be infidels, or gods of stone or wood
If man had kept the Sabbath day the way God said he should.
He doesn't ask for all our time, just one day of the week.
Of all the days He's given us, the seventh we should keep.
This Friday when the sun has set, put earthly cares away.
Just spend these sacred hours with God and keep His holy day.

Honor thy father and thy mother that thy days may be long
upon the land which the Lord thy God giveth thee

HONOR YOUR PARENTS

Honor your father and mother. Respect them in every way.
Show them the love that is due them. You'll surely prolong your days.
When they are old and enfeebled, they need all your love and care.
Kindness comes back when it's given, with blessings beyond compare.
Parents don't claim to be perfect. At times they may come unglued.
Sometimes decisions are faulty and motives are misconstrued.
God said obey them regardless, as long as it's in the Lord.
This is the right type of conduct. It comes from His Holy Word.

Thou shalt not kill

TAKING A LIFE

In this society today, there's too much war and strife.
It's almost nothing for some thug to take another's life.
But God said you should never kill. Don't wield that gun or knife.
A person must be pretty low to take another's life.
And God said even if you hate another without strife,
That you'd be charged with murder, just as though you took his life.
Let's put away all evil thoughts, all angry words and strife.
We must show love to everyone to gain eternal life

Thou shalt not commit adultery

GOD'S PRECIOUS GIFT

God said it wasn't good for man that he should be alone.
So He presented him with love, made from his very bone.
He put within emotions that would make their flesh as one.
The more they used this precious gift the closer they'd become.
But Satan got inside man's thoughts, and caused him to digress.
And sin stepped in, perverted it, and caused an awful mess.
So many broken families, so many tears are shed,
Because the vows are broken and so many lies are spread.
Abortions now are rampant, and diseases take their toll.
The world is full of pain and strife because man lost control.
God doesn't take it lightly when you bring about this shame.
Respect this gift He's given you, and glorify His name.

Thou shalt not steal.

HIGHER STANDARDS

Most Christians would not even think to take what is not theirs.
For they would never rob nor steal-not even on a dare.
When sticky fingers take control, it's time to kneel and pray,
For God said stealing is a sin, a crime for which we'll pay.
But some things go unnoticed when unwittingly we rob,
Like getting paid for precious moments wasted on the job,
Or failing to report income that's due the IRS,
Or lying on a resume to help us gain success.
And when we keep back any of the tithe that's due to God,
We're robbing Him, the Bible says, and guilty of a fraud.
As Christians, we must always lift standards above the world.
By living higher than the norm, Christ's banner we'll unfurl.

Thou shalt not bear false witness.

LYING

Lies come in many varied forms, little fibs or outright lies.
They may provoke a hearty laugh or at times, demoralize.
Sometimes it's hard for us to see that a fib is still a lie.
When we don't want to go someplace, we begin to falsify.
If we don't want to do some thing we create an alibi.
We make excuses right and left, but a fib is still a lie.
Sometimes our words can be quite cruel when the lies are magnified.
When others change them just a bit, our false statements multiply.
Don't spread that rumor you just heard, for you might be spreading lies.
Don't even think an evil thought for it could be verbalized.
God said to always speak the truth. Lying lips disgust our Lord.
Unless we speak our words in truth we will reap our just reward.

Thou shalt not covet.

ENVY

Sometimes we meet a person "green with envy," so to speak.
He's always discontented for he has a selfish streak.
He wants to be admired by his multitude of friends.
He needs to be looked up to, so he always sets the trends.
If someone should outshine him with a house or brand new car
His face turns green with envy, for he has to be the star.
Don't let another's talent supersede his aptitude!
Then envy looms within him and he'll sit around and brood.
When envy gets inside you it creates a lot of strife.
Praise God for all His blessings. Be contented with your life.

MARY AND JOSEPH

There once was a couple in Nazareth engaged to be married one day.
When Joseph found out things weren't normal, he wanted to put her away.
An angel said, "Joseph, don't do that, for Mary conceived all alone.
Except for some help from the Spirit, her Child is the Father's own Son."
They married, and when it was tax time, they started to travel one day.
They slept in an old rustic stable, because there was no place to stay.
That night, Jesus made His appearance. There wasn't a crib for His head.
He had to lie down with the cattle, and sleep in a manger instead.
The angels announced to the shepherds attending their sheep on a hill,
That Jesus was born in a stable in Bethlehem, when all was still.
The Wise men looked up and acknowledged the star they had seen overhead.
They purchased some gifts for the Baby, and followed the star where it led.
Then Joseph took Mary and Jesus and went into Egypt awhile,
Because Herod's heart was so wicked. He wanted to kill the Christ Child.
When Joseph was certain that Herod was no longer king on the throne,
The family then traveled to Nazareth to Mary and Joseph's old home.
And Jesus waxed strong in the Spirit. God's grace was abundant with Him.
And there He increased in all knowledge, in favor with God and with men.

THE PASSOVER

When Jesus reached the age of twelve, he heard His father say,
"Let's travel to Jerusalem to keep this Holy Day."
And when Passover ended, it was time to travel home.
They didn't realize that Christ was not among His own.
Back to Jerusalem they went to find their missing Boy.
And when at last they found Him, how their hearts were filled with joy.
Among the Doctors and the Scribes they found this youthful Lad,
Astounding them with questions and with answers that He had.
And when His mother said, "You made us look through all the land."
He said, "I do God's business, now, why don't you understand?"
And Christ waxed strong in Spirit and God's grace remained with Him.
His wisdom did increase, and He found favor with all men.

CHRIST'S BAPTISM

Christ's cousin, John the Baptist, preached repentance for all sin.
He was the Voice that cried aloud, "Prepare the way for Him."
When people asked him if he were the Christ, he did reply,
"No, He's the mighty Son of God. His shoes I can't untie."
The Jordan beckoned John one day. Christ came to be baptized.
"Behold the Lamb of God!" John said. His Lord he recognized.
A Dove came down upon Him. God said, "I'm pleased with You.
You are My own beloved Son." His strength He did renew.

THE TEMPTATION

Christ went into the wilderness to prove that right can win.
For forty days He ate no food, his face was pale and thin.
When He was starving and quite weak, who came to visit Him?
This dazzling, but deceptive foe--looked like a cherubim.
"If You're the Son of God," he said, "pick up this smooth round stone
And make a tasty loaf of bread, all for Your very own."
"You know that man cannot survive on bread alone," Christ said.
"It takes the precious Word of God, along with daily bread."
And then the devil carried Him up to a mountain high.
"If You'll bow down and worship me, all this is Yours," he cried.
"O, Satan, get behind My back. The Bible says that we
Should worship God, and God alone, and serve Him faithfully."
Then Satan carried Jesus to the Temple, where he said,
"Jump off! God will not let You fall. He'll lift You up instead."
And Jesus answered him again, "Don't tempt God with your plot."
And Satan slithered out of sight. His mission now was shot.
Christ lost what energy He had. He thought He'd surely faint.
An angel came to nourish Him and give Him back His strength.
Out there in that forsaken place, Christ proved it's possible
To shun the devil and his schemes. God's word is powerful!

THE MARRIAGE AT CANA

In Cana there was a wedding, and Jesus was asked to be there.
The guests began to assemble, and happiness soon filled the air.
The wine was better than usual, and people drank more than their share,
And soon it dwindled to nothing. The host was then filled with despair.
Then Mary, Jesus' own mother stepped forward and said to her Son,
"My Son, the host has a problem. He's frantic! The wine is all gone."
Then Jesus answered His mother and said, "Mom, My hour has not come.
I'll do what's needed, however. The problem is quite troublesome.
"You see those water pots standing? They're empty and need to be filled."
The servants left in a hurry, and hastened to do Jesus' will.
Then Jesus said to the servants, "The governor would like some to drink."
And when he tasted, he marveled, "Just why are You doing this thing?
The best wine always is given at first 'til the guests have their fill.
But you have saved the best grape juice 'til last, and it really excels!"
Now turning water to grape juice, to us, is a pretty big thing.
It's done each day on the grapevine. For Him, it's a simple routine.

THE SYRO-PHOENICIAN WOMAN

When Jesus departed to Tyre, a woman of Canaan was there.
"My daughter's possessed with a devil. It's something that I cannot bear."
But Jesus ignored this poor woman. His friends said, "Just send her away."
But Christ said, "I have a great mission to save souls in Israel today."
Then Jesus said to the woman, "My bread doesn't go to the dogs."
"The dogs lick the crumbs that have fallen," she said in this short dialog.
"Oh, woman, your faith is outstanding. Your daughter is healed this same hour.
Because of your faith I have helped her, and she has received of My power."
He did this to teach His disciples that no one's an outcast with Him.
All people, regardless of background are pardoned and cleansed from their sin.

THE BLIND BEGGAR

One day Jesus went down to Jericho. A multitude followed close by.
A blind man sat begging and heard them pass,
"What's happening?" That blind man did cry.
"Oh, Jesus of Nazareth passes by." The blind man then yelled out to Him,
"Please Jesus, have mercy upon my soul." "Be quiet!" The crowd said to him.
Again he said, "Jesus have mercy, now." And Jesus said, "Bring Me the man.
Just what do you want Me to do for you?" "Please give me my sight once again."
And Christ said, "Your eyes shall be opened, now.
Your faith really caused you to see."
He glorified Jesus of Nazareth. The multitude praised Him with glee.

FEEDING THE FIVE THOUSAND

Jesus went up on a mountain. He noticed a crowd coming near.
Since it was evening, He pondered, "How will we get food to them here?"
Andrew said, "There is a young lad with two fish and five loaves of bread."
"Ask him if he would be willing to share it with Me," Jesus said.
"Master, You know I am willing to share my two fish and the bread."
Many sat down in small circles, and my, what a table He spread!
Christ blessed the food that He borrowed, fed five thousand people that day,
Took up twelve baskets remaining. God's glory was put on display.

THE MAN BORN BLIND

One Sabbath as Jesus was walking, he saw a man blind from his birth.
"Whose fault is this?" Said His disciples. "His parents? His lack of self-worth?"
"Nobody's at fault," said the Master, "I came here to glorify God."
And after a small dissertation, He stooped down and spat on the sod.
He picked up the wet sand and molded some clay to be put on his eyes.
"Go wash in the pool of Saloam, your sight you will soon realize."
"Who did this?" The Pharisees asked him. "They tell me it's Jesus," he said.
"He may not be truthful and honest, we'll talk to his parents instead."
"Has this man been blind from a baby?" they asked of his parents that day.
"How is it, his eyes have been opened?" "Ask him. Our son knows what to say."
Some people said, "This Man's a sinner, for He broke the Sabbath today."
"How can He be sinful and do this? You'd think that this Man was OK."
Again, the once-blind man was questioned. "He's sinful. Now don't you agree?"
"I only know I was in darkness. I thank God, that now I can see."

THE POOL OF BETHESDA

When Jesus went up to Jerusalem, He went near the sheep market, there.
A pool called Bethesda was crowded with some people bogged down in despair.
They figured an angel descended there to heal the first one in the pool.
The quick and the greedy surrounded it, to see who was first to be fooled.
A man who was crippled and needed help, just lay there for thirty-eight years.
And Jesus walked up and said,
"Friend, do you want healing and strength in here?"
"Oh, Master, there's no one to help me, now. I can't make it into the pool.
The quick and the agile all beat me there. I'm downcast and quite sorrowful."
And Jesus said, "Take up your bed and walk,
for strength has now come to your soul."
Rejoicing, he walked through Jerusalem, For Jesus had made this man whole.

WALKING ON THE WATER

When Jesus told His disciples, "I'm going to the mountain to pray,"
His friends got into a small boat and they started sailing away.
A storm arose on the water. The winds almost blew them apart.
They wished that Jesus were with them to comfort their poor trembling hearts.
They looked and saw something moving. Of course, they were not very brave.
They thought a ghost was evolving, and walking out there on the waves.
Then Jesus called His disciples, "Now don't be afraid. It is I."
And Peter said to the Master, "Let me come and give it a try."
"Oh, yes," said Jesus to Peter, "Come walk on the water with Me."
And out of the boat Peter ventured. His friends were as shocked as could be.
He took his eyes off the Master and looked at the waves all around.
And when his feet started sinking, he thought he was going to drown.
"Oh save me, Jesus. I'm sinking!" And then Jesus put out His hand.
"Now, Peter, why did you doubt Me? Your faith has been weakened, My man."
And when they stepped in the sail boat the winds ceased to blow them around.
And all His friends in that vessel kneeled down as they worshiped God's Son.

JESUS RAISES LAZARUS

There once was a sick man named Lazarus, a friend of the Master, I'd say.
His sisters, then sent word to Jesus and said, "Lazarus needs You today."
But Jesus said, "Please do not worry, God's glory must be on display."
He tarried, and lingered awhile, and then said, "Let's be on our way."
And when they arrived, Martha met Him. "Just why did you linger, my Lord?
My brother is dead. Aren't you troubled? His sickness, You chose to ignore.
"I know that whatever You ask for, God gives You. I'm sure You'll agree."
"Your brother shall rise. Don't you worry. Existence and life come from Me."
Then Mary fell down and was prostrate. "I don't know why he had to die."
And Jesus was saddened and troubled so much that He started to cry.
He went to the grave and commanded, "Please take that stone out of the way."
"Oh no, Lord, his flesh is decaying. He's been there, already, four days.
"I'm sure that by now he smells rotten," his sister proceeded to say.
"Just do as I say," Jesus answered. "God's glory will shine forth today."
Then Jesus said, "Lazarus, come out here!" And Lazarus obeyed His command.
"Please loose him, unwrap all his grave clothes."
And Lazarus walked off, a new man.

THE WIDOW OF NAIN

One day Jesus went to a town called Nain and watched as a funeral went by.
This woman's dear son, and her only son, had died, and she started to cry.
"Don't cry, little lady, I've hope for you." And Jesus went up to the lad.
"Arise, My young fellow, and live again." He woke up and made his mom glad.

THE TEN LEPERS

One day Jesus went to a village. Ten lepers stood off to the side.
They lifted their voices and called Him, "Have mercy! Oh, Master," they cried.
And Jesus took pity upon them. He cleansed them and made their flesh whole.
"Go now, so the Priest can behold you, and give you a blessing, untold."
The lepers were cured as they traveled. Their flesh became pink once again.
But only one man turned to thank Him, although Jesus knew He cleansed ten.

THE WILD MAN

When Christ and His disciples sailed across the lake one day,
A wild, ferocious mental case came out in disarray.
No one could even chain him down. He cut himself with stones
'Til blood gushed out and flesh was torn, right to the very bone.
He recognized the Master and he fell upon his knee.
He said, "Oh, Son of God on High, I pray, don't torment me."
Christ told the evil spirits that they had to leave him, then.
"Please send us to that herd of swine that we may enter them."
"All right, possess that herd of swine, I'll listen to your plea."
Immediately the pigs went wild and jumped into the sea.

THE MAN WITH PALSY

Another man stricken with palsy had wanted to see Christ one day.
Too many had come and the small house was crowded, much to his dismay.
They took him up high on a roof-top, and dug out a neat little hole.
They lowered his bed down to Jesus so he could accomplish his goal.
The Master at once knew the problem. "Your sins are forgiven," He cried.
"He can't forgive sins," people whispered. But Christ seemed to take it in stride.
He answered, "Why haggle among you if I can forgive sins, or heal?
The Son gets His power from heaven. God's love I'll display and reveal."
He turned to the man sick with palsy, "Please rise, take your bed with you, too."
He got up and went on rejoicing. Christ made all his wishes come true.

JAIRUS' DAUGHTER & THE ISSUE OF BLOOD

While Christ was walking, many folks came out to welcome Him.
A ruler of the synagogue stepped forth. His face was grim.
And at the feet of Jesus did this lofty ruler bow,
For Jairus' daughter almost died. She needed help, somehow.
"Please come and put Your hands on her that she may be made whole."
And Jesus rose and followed him to heal this precious soul.
But on the way He was delayed, the crowd was pretty thick.
A woman touched His garment's hem, for she was pretty sick.
She didn't want to be made known, humiliated by
This thing that so embarrassed her, and made her very shy.
But Christ said, "Who reached out to Me? Somebody touched My hem."
His friends said, "All these people here, and You felt one of them?"
But Christ said, "Power went out of Me. I felt it leave My soul."
He knew that virtue flowed from Him and made this woman whole.
And yet, while He conversed with her, poor Jairus' daughter died.
"There's no need for the Master, now," the servant did confide.
"Don't be afraid," Christ said to him. "We still will travel on.
Not everyone can go with Me, just Peter, James and John."
When they arrived, the noise was great. Folks cried and moaned aloud.
"Why do you stand around and weep?" Christ asked this mournful crowd.
"The girl is sleeping. She's not dead," Christ tried to comfort them.
My how they laughed and scorned His words. They mocked and mimicked Him.
But Christ sent all of them away, except her mom and dad,
And Peter, James, and John went in. Nobody, now, was sad.
Christ took the maiden by the hand and said, "Stand up, My child.
Give her some food, she's hungry now." And everybody smiled

TWO BLIND MEN

After leaving Jairus' home two blind men came to Him.
"Son of David, touch us now!" And Jesus said to them,
"Tell me, do you think that I can do this for your soul?"
"Yes, we know Your power, Lord." And Jesus made them whole.
"Don't tell anyone of this," the Master cautioned them.
Soon as He was out of sight, they spread it to all men.

THE STORM

Christ and His twelve disciples stepped in a boat one day.
Christ went to sleep, and shortly, the bright clouds turned to gray.
The sky kept getting darker, a tempest did arise.
The boat went helter-skelter. They thought it would capsize.
They went to find the Master. "How can You sleep through this?
The waves are tossing 'round us and water's in our midst."
"My friends, why are you fearful? Your faith is kind of weak!"
And Jesus calmed the tempest. The waters did recede.

THE WITHERED HAND

One Sabbath in the synagogue, a man was standing there.
He had a limp and withered hand. Few people seemed to care.
The Pharisees then tried their best to trip the Savior up.
"On Sabbath, can you heal a man and not be called corrupt?"
He once again out-smarted them and said to that small crowd,
"If your sheep fell into the pit, you'd try to get him out.
And even on the Sabbath Day, it's lawful to do good."
He healed that limp and withered hand. No one misunderstood.

THE BLIND AND SPEECHLESS MAN

A man was brought to Jesus who was blind and could not speak.
They said he had a devil, which, I'm sure, was not unique.
"Is this the Son of David?" All the Pharisees did say.
"The devil made Him do it, for there is no other way."
But Jesus knew their thinking. He chastised those hypocrites.
He gave them quite a sermon on their stratagem and wit.

THE CENTURION'S SERVANT

Christ traveled to Capernaum. A man was in despair.
He was a kind Centurion with lots of love and care.
"Please make my servant well again, for palsy's got him down."
And Jesus said, "Let's go to him, I'll make his body sound.

"O no! You needn't come with me, just speak the word alone.
And Jesus said, "Your faith is strong. Consider it as done."
And at the very self-same hour the palsied man was healed.
Because his master's faith was strong he saw God's love revealed.

THE BEATITUDES

Jesus then taught His disciples many things they could comprehend.
Going up high on a mountain He expounded these truths to them.
Blessed are those poor in spirit, for the Kingdom belongs to them.
Blessed are those who are mournful, they'll be comforted once again.
Blessed are all of the meek ones, for the earth has been promised them.
Blessed are those who are hungry for God's Word, they will comprehend.
Blessed are those who show mercy, for in turn, they'll receive it, too.
Blessed are those who are spotless, for God's face they will get to view.
Blessed are those who are peaceful. They are children of God on High.
Blessed are those persecuted, for the Kingdom they'll occupy.
Blessed are those who are falsely and maliciously lied upon,
Many rewards will be given. They'll see God and His precious Son.

THE LIFE OF CHRIST

Christ's life was one of wonders, for He did so many things
To help the ones around Him, and relieve their suffering.
He healed the broken-hearted, and He set the captives free.
He healed the sick and wounded, blessed the children on His knee.
He went through towns and cities touching people where they lay.
He comforted the hurting, making friends along the way.
Each day was spent in service all around the neighborhood.
He gave His life for others, and was always doing good.
Why would the King of Glory leave His Father's courts above?
The only explanation is, He came because of love.
We needed reconciling. For this world was lost in sin.
He came to offer pardon and to win us back to Him.

THE SACRIFICIAL LAMB

The Bible tells a story of an undisputed love.
The God of all the universe left heaven's courts above.
The King of all the world became The Man of Galilee.
I can't begin to understand His love for you and me.
Of one thing I am certain, and I'm sure that you'll agree.
There is no one so loving as this Man of Galilee.
We can't begin to understand the love He has for man.
Was there a reason why He came? Some designated plan?
Why would He give His life for me and shed His precious blood?
There is no other reason, than, He came because of love.
It was decided long ago before this world began   ,
If man should sin, Christ would become The Sacrificial Lamb.
When Mary had this little Lamb, His heart was white as snow.
And everywhere that Mary went, the Lamb was sure to go.
He followed her to church each week. He learned the Golden Rule,
She taught Him Scripture at her knee, that was His only school.
He came to live and dwell on earth that I might be set free.
He came to offer pardon, so He shed His blood for me.
Christ knew there was no other way. It was His only plan.
I love to hear the story of this Sacrificial Lamb.

THE PASSOVER FEAST

When Christ's disciples came to Him, Passover time was near.
"We must prepare the feast," they said. "Where will we go this year?"
"Go find this man and say to him, 'Your house we want to use
To celebrate this holy feast.' He'll surely not refuse."
That evening when the sun had set, Christ sat down with His friends
To eat this sacred, holy meal as God did recommend.
And as they ate, Christ said aloud, "An evil deed is planned,
For someone will betray Me, now, and get the upper hand."
Of course they looked inside their souls, and some of them did cry,
"O who would do this awful thing? My Lord, could it be I?"
He answered them and said these words, "Whoever dips his hand
And puts it in the dish with Me betrays the Son of Man.
It's written, I must suffer, and My duty I'll perform.
But he who would betray Me now, should never have been born."
Then Judas turned to Him and said, "O Master, is it I?"
"The finger points to you, My man," the Master did reply.
Then Jesus blessed the bread He held and gave some to each man.
"This is My Body," Jesus said, "Please eat this Paschal lamb."
He also put His blessings on the cup that held the wine.
"This is My blood that I will shed to rescue all mankind."
They sang a song, then, left the room to go upon the mount.
"You'll be ashamed of Me," Christ said, "when enemies surround."
And Peter said, "I'll never be ashamed of You, my Lord,
Though all these others let You down. I've given You my word."
" Of course, Christ had to say to him, "Before the cock crows twice
You'll be so much ashamed of Me that you'll deny Me thrice."
"I'd die before I let You down!" The others did agree.
These famous words that Peter spoke went down in history,

GETHSEMANE

A nice secluded spot was found, it was Gethsemane.
Christ told His friends, "Please sit down here while I take only three."
And taking Peter, James and John, He said, "What can I do?
My soul is heavy unto death, I need support from you."
He went a little farther on, fell on His face to pray,
"O God, if it be possible, please, take this cup away."
The agony was so intense, great drops of blood were shed.
"O Father, listen to My plea! Deliver Me," He said.
"I do not want to go through this. Please find another way.
But I will put My trust in You. Your will I must obey."
How much support did these men give when Christ began to weep?
Three times He came for comfort and He found them fast asleep.
"Get up," Christ said, "you've slept enough. You should have prayed instead.
I've been betrayed. It's over now. Let's face what lies ahead."
For while He prayed old Judas had to show his evil hand.
For thirty coins of silver He betrayed the Son of Man.
He haggled with some evil men at least once, maybe twice,
'Til all of them were satisfied, and came up with this price.
Then Judas brought an angry mob to this secluded place.
The kiss of death was planted on the Master's careworn face.
They laid their hands on Jesus as He said, "Why are you here?"
And Peter tried to slit one's throat, but only got his ear.
Christ took that mutilated ear and showed His power to heal.
He said to Peter, "Take your sword. That's not for you to wield.
I don't need help," Christ said to him. "For if I did, you see,
Twelve legions of My Father's hosts would come and rescue Me.
The Scriptures long ago foretold that this must be," He said.
When all His followers heard that, they turned around and fled.
Before the trial, that sleazy one who sold Him to the priests
Reflected on his evil deed, and he was none too pleased.
He took the money back to them and threw it at their feet.
And then went out and hanged himself, because of his misdeed.

CAIAPHAS

When Caiaphas said, "Bring Him to me. I'll take Him for awhile."
False witnesses were then brought forth--made mockery of the trial.
When asked to give an answer to the charges facing Him,
Christ held His peace, said not a word. The Priest was wroth within.
"You'll answer me and do it now! Are you the Son of God?"
"You said it right. You soon will see Me coming on a cloud."
The High Priest tore his garment, then. "You've blasphemed God," he said.
"The proof that we were seeking can be found in what You said."
When Peter saw them spit on Christ and slap Him in the face,
He mingled with the jeering crowd, too scared to show his face.
A little girl came up to him, "You're Jesus' friend," she cried.
"O no!" scared Peter said to her. His Lord he did deny.
He quickly went onto the porch. A maid then forced his hand.
"You're this Man's friend." And Peter said, "I never saw that Man!"
The people standing near the porch off from the corridor
Said Peter's speech betrayed him, so old Peter cursed and swore.
As Peter heard the rooster crow, his heart felt numb inside.
When Jesus turned and looked at him, he hung his head and cried.
His heart cried out, "Forgive me Lord. I'm lost! What can I do?"
Christ's tender look of love told him, "I have forgiven you."

PILATE'S JUDGMENT HALL

The Priest took Christ to Pilate, followed by the angry throng.
"What are the charges?" Pilate said. "Just what did He do wrong?"
"He fed the hungry people and He made the blind to see.
He healed the sick and raised the dead, and calmed the raging sea.
He helped the poor and needy, blessed the children on His knee.
The deaf can understand Him, now. He's filled with blasphemy."
"This Man did not commit a crime. He needs to be set free.
I find no fault with Him at all. I'm sure that you'll agree.
I know this Man is innocent!" The crowd heard Pilate scream.
"An angel even told my wife. Last night she had a dream.
I must release a prisoner. Someone will be set free.
Should I release Barabbas or this Man of Galilee?"
"We want Barabbas to go free. Yes, set Barabbas free.
He lied, he stole, he murdered, but we want him to go free.
We want Barabbas to go free. Yes, set Barabbas free.
We'd rather have a robber than this Man of Galilee."
"Barabbas is a murderer! This Christ has done no wrong.
Yet you insist you want Him free. Why are you so headstrong?
What should I do with Jesus if I set Barabbas free?
I'm through with Him. What should I do to Christ of Galilee?"
"Just crucify this rebel. We won't listen to your plea.
Just crucify this evil one. Don't let this Man go free."
So Pilate turned Him over to that cruel wicked crowd.
They beat Him 'til the blood gushed out, put thorns upon His brow.
They stripped His garments as they mocked, "Hail to the King of Jews."
They cleared their throats and spat on Him.
It thrilled them through and through.
They put a cross upon His back on that Golgotha Road.
The weight was more than He could bear. He fell beneath the load.

THE CROSS

They nailed Christ to a cruel tree and pierced Him in the side.
His blood ran like a river. My sins caused Him to die.
Two thieves were nailed beside our Lord. One said, "Remember me.
I want to go to Paradise. Please cleanse and set me free."
Then Jesus turned His face toward him and said to him that day,
"You'll be with Me in heaven for your sins are washed away."
They gave Him vinegar to drink, because His mouth was dry.
He said, "Father, forgive them." And He bowed His head and died.
And in the temple where the Priest would slay another lamb,
The temple veil was rent in two, torn by an unseen hand.
The earth began to shake and reel, the sky was dark as night.
The air grew cold and chilly when the sun concealed its light.
The angels veiled their faces. All nature seemed to moan.
The Father turned His back on Him. He bore it all alone.
Then Joseph took His body down, placed it in his new tomb.
The Roman soldiers sealed it shut that Friday afternoon.
The tomb became His resting place that Sabbath long ago
When Christ redeemed this fallen world, what love He did bestow,

RESURRECTION MORNING

When early Sunday morning came, God said, "Go call My Son."
And Gabriel's feet hit solid clay. An earthquake shook the ground.
The Roman soldiers at the tomb fell back like they were dead.
The sight of just one angel knocked them down, the Scripture said.
The heavy stone just rolled away. Christ rose triumphantly.
The grave could not contain my Lord, Who gave His life for me.
O Glory! Hallelujah! Jesus died to save my soul.
He gave His life to ransom me. Now I have been made whole.
Because He holds the keys of death and rose victoriously
I'll live with Him forevermore throughout eternity.

WORTH IT ALL

Christ bled and died that you might live. You caused Him grief and pain.
Have you accepted Him today, or was His death in vain?
I want to take you back in time when Christ took all your blame,
When Jesus suffered in your place and bore your guilt and shame.
Think of the beatings that He took, the slaps, the hits, the blows,
The lacerations on His back that caused His blood to flow.
Think of His nail-pierced hands and feet, the pain on that cruel tree.
Think of the shame that He endured, unclothed for all to see.
Just think of what He did for you to wipe your sins away.
He gave His life! Was it in vain? Your penalty He paid.
Christ said, "I gave My all for you. For you I shed My blood.
I gladly suffered for your sake. I did it out of love."
Don't let His dying be in vain. Please give your heart to Him.
Christ died for you that you might live. He'll wash away your sins.
And when you get to heaven and eternal life you gain,
He'll say, "What I went through for you, was truly worth the pain."

JESUS

He's the Lovely Rose of Sharon. He's the Bright and Morning Star.
He's the Fairest of Ten Thousand, and He loves us as we are.
He's the Vine and we're the branches, He's the perfect, spotless Lamb,
He's the Bread that came from heaven, and He is the great I Am.
He's the Water ever flowing. He's the Mighty Prince of Peace.
He's the Everlasting Father, and He is our great High Priest.
He is love beyond all measure. He is merciful and true,
He is gracious and longsuffering, and He wants to be with you.
He is pleading, gently pleading. Won't you open up your heart?
He is willing to forgive you and His grace He will impart.

THE PRODIGAL SON

The younger son on one estate was bored with all the rules,
Was tired of plowing, growing grain, and sick of cows and mules.
"Please give me what is due me, now. I'm going it alone.
It's like I'm in a prison house. I'll make it on my own."
And so he took his newfound wealth and squandered it away
On girls and booze, just having fun, 'til it was gone one day.
He ended up among the pigs and ate their husks and cobs.
"I'm going to my father's house. He'll offer me a job."
Each day his father waited for his younger son's return.
And when he saw him down the road, his heart began to burn.
New clothes were put upon his back, new shoes upon his feet.
A feast was made on his behalf. Their union was complete.
But what about the older son whose heart was burdened down
Because he labored faithfully? He seemed to wear a frown.
But then the father said to him, "You're loyal, firm and true.
My son, you've always stayed with me. My wealth belongs to you.
Your younger brother once was lost, where family was concerned.
But with God's help he found himself and now he has returned."
My friend, have you gone on your own and left your Father's place?
He's waiting now for your return. Accept His love and grace.

THE PHARISEE AND PUBLICAN

The Pharisee and the Publican went into the Temple to pray.
The Pharisee squared his shoulders back and here's what he started to say.
"Oh, Lord, I am thankful I don't sin like this man who's praying here, too.
And others are evil and wicked, adulterers, cheaters, untrue."
The Publican touched his humble breast, acknowledging he was in sin.
"Have mercy, my Father. Touch me now. I know what a sinner I've been."
Don't gloat over having righteousness. It shows you are missing your goal.
Admit you're a sinner saved by grace. Let God take control of your soul.

THE GOOD SAMARITAN

A man was on a lonely road near Jericho one day.
Some thugs with mischief in their eyes were looking for a prey.
They did some dreadful things to him, beat, bruised, and blacked his eye.
They robbed him of his bag of gold and left him there to die.
A priest came by and looked at him, then went his merry way.
He had important business there, in Jericho that day.
A Levite also came along, crossed to the other side.
The man would surely be unclean, especially if he died.
A Good Samaritan came by and soothed his wounds with oil.
He put the man upon his mule, although his clothes would soil.
He took him to the nearest inn, paid for his room and care,
And told the keeper at the door, all extra he would bear.
It is your Christian duty to show mercy to all men,
To help your neighbor when in need and be to him a friend.

THE VINEYARD

A certain man planted a vineyard, and pruned it, and worked it with care.
He rented it to a few farmers, then left to go travel elsewhere.
And when the fruit flourished and ripened, his servants were sent to receive
The fruit that was ready for harvest, and see what the farmers achieved.
Instead of receiving the harvest, the husbandmen beat, killed and stoned
Those servants who wanted to gather the fruit that the master had sown.
Again, he sent others to gather the fruit from the ground that was tilled.
The husbandmen acted with malice, they beat one, and stoned one and killed.
"They'll reverence my son if I send him," the master decided that day.
He didn't know they were so wicked. They killed him and tossed him away.
It doesn't take much to determine the fate of those farmers that day.
I'm sure they received a just sentence, although the account doesn't say.
For years people treated with malice God's prophets, since time had begun.
They killed them, mistreated and stoned them, and even rejected His Son.
It doesn't take much to determine the sinner's demise. We are told
They'll burn in the fires of destruction when end time events all unfold.

THE WHEAT AND THE TARES

A man sowed good seed in his field one day,
then lay down to sleep for the night.
An enemy entered the new-sown field and planted some weeds,
then took flight.
When sunshine and rain caused the seeds to grow,
there also appeared all the weeds.
The servants said, "Master, your seed was good.
What man did this dastardly deed?"
The master replied, "I am positive an enemy did this bad thing."
"Let's pull out the weeds, sir," the servants said,
"so only good fruit it will bring."
"Oh no!" said the master. "You can't do that.
You might pull up some of the best.
When ripe, we will gather the weeds to burn, and then we will harvest the rest."
In God's field are people we think are weeds, but we can't be certain or sure.
He'll gather the weeds to be tied and burned, and save only those who are pure.

THE TALENTS

Before one man went on a journey, his servants came at his request.
He said, "I am leaving this country." And gave them his goods to invest.
Each servant received something different, according to what he could do.
One servant received just one talent, one five, and another just two.
The man with five talents invested, and doubled the goods he received.
And likewise, the man with two talents was happy with what he achieved.
The servant receiving one talent decided to hide the man's worth.
He went out and dug in the soil, and buried it under the earth.
And when it was time for the master to call them to his corridor,
The servant with five talents smiled for he had brought five talents more.
The man with two talents was cheerful. His talents had doubled with ease.
They both received blessings and honor. The master was happy and pleased.
The man with one talent said, "Master, I know you're a hard driving soul.
I took that one talent you gave me and buried it deep in a hole".
"You're wicked, lethargic and lazy. You should have invested with men.
I'll take the one talent I gave you and give it to him who has ten."
We all have received a few talents. Let's use them to further God's cause.
The more that we use, He will double. And we will receive His applause.

THE LABORERS

"I need someone to tend my fields," a man declared one day.
"The fruit is ripe. I need some help. If you will work, I'll pay."
The master and the laborers agreed upon a price.
"We'll work for you 'til day is done. The pay is pretty nice."
And later on, he asked more men to help him in the field.
The same amount was offered them. They said it was a deal.
And just before the setting sun he found men out of work.
"We can't find one to hire us," they said with quite a smirk.
And even though the hour was late, the deal was still the same.
"Oh yes, my lord. We'll work for you," those loafers did exclaim.
When pay-up time had come around, each got the same amount.
"It isn't fair!" The first group cried. "Your actions are unsound."
"I paid you what we settled on," the master did reply.
"Take what is yours and go your way. Why stand around and cry?"
For all who will confess their sins, and call upon His name,
Eternal life is their reward. The wages are the same.

THE TREASURES

A man was working in a field, when much to his surprise,
He found a precious treasure there. He must have been quite wise.
The field did not belong to him, so what was he to do?
"I'll buy that field," the toiler said. "I'll own the treasure, too.
I need to make adjustments, so the treasure I can claim.
I'll need to sell all that I own to get it in my name."
Another man sold all he had to buy one priceless pearl.
He may have sold his diamonds or some rubies and his beryl.
How much will you be willing, now, to go through stress and strife,
To claim the precious promises and gain eternal life?

THE SOWER

A man decided to plant some seeds. He scattered them all around.
They landed in and around the field, on barren and fertile ground.
Some seeds decided to go astray. The birds ate them one by one.
And some just landed among the stones. They died in the scorching sun.
Some seeds were sprinkled among the thorns.
The thorns simply choked them out.
The seeds that fell on the fertile ground had hundreds of sturdy sprouts.
Each day we're constantly sowing seeds by things that we do and say.
Good fruit will flourish and multiply when nurtured by Christ each day.

THE ROYAL FEAST

A certain man prepared a feast, fit for a royal king.
He told his servant to go out and tell what's happening.
"Come to the feast my lord prepared. You cannot do without."
"I'm sorry, but I bought some land that I must see about."
"I bought some oxen," one man said. "I have to try them out."
A newly-wed said, "Sorry Sir, my wife would cry and pout."
The servant's master was not pleased when he was told this thing.
"Invite the poor, the lame, the blind. I'll feed all that you bring.
"Go far and wide," the master said. "There is much room to spare.
Compel the folks to fill my house, all people everywhere."
The servants, then, were told to go to highways, fields and country.
Invite the good, bad, old and young, the gluttons and the hungry.
The king prepared a formal gown to clothe the guests in splendor.
One man refused to wear his robe, was labeled an offender.
Of course, they bound him hand and foot, because he couldn't tell them
Why he refused the wedding gown. This man became a felon.
Christ has a banquet just for you. What reason do you give
Why you would rather do your thing, than look to Him and live?

THE RICH MAN WITH PLENTY

A rich man had plenty of harvest, but no place to store it away.
He should have been looking for someone who needed some food for that day.
Instead, he was greedy and selfish. He looked at his barns where they stood.
"I'll tear down and build bigger silos to store all my fruits and my goods."
He knew he was rich and had plenty, and smugly he said with a smile,
"I'll eat it, and drink and be happy. My pantry is full for awhile."
But God said, "You're foolish and wicked. You've come to the end of your time.
Your barns that are loaded with produce are wasted and not worth a dime."
Don't hoard what you have to get wealthy. Too many are hungry and cold.
Reach out with some tender compassion, and you will have riches untold.

THE LOST SHEEP

A little lamb strayed from the fold, lost in the darkest night.
He trembled, shivered and was cold, longing to see the light.
The shepherd must have cringed that night, leaving his precious sheep
To find the frightened baby lamb, after they went to sleep.
And after searching for awhile, calling the lamb by name,
He found the baby, picked him up, easing his fear and pain.
He put the baby on his neck, carried him to the fold.
Then nurtured, fed, and cared for him, giving him love untold.
Are you out there in sin and shame, lost in the darkest night?
The Master's looking for you now to bring you love and light.

THE WEDDING FEAST

A certain king prepared a feast. His son was getting married.
His servant called his friends to come, but everybody tarried.
Another servant then called out, "The marriage supper's ready."
One person laughed. He had to farm his private land. How petty!
Another checked his purchased goods. I guess he sorted through them.
And some responded spitefully. They took those men and slew them.
Now when the king received the news, his soul was filled with furor.
He struck them dead and burned their towns, because they delved in murder.
When Christ asked you to dine with Him, did you respond with favor?
Or did you carelessly decide to spurn the loving Savior?
The invitation still goes out. Will you accept with pleasure?
Or like those thugs, will you receive His fury without measure?

THE TWO HOUSES

Two men decided to build a house. The wiser one built on a rock.
He dug until he made sure it was the safest house there on the block.
The other man didn't plan too well, his house was built on the sand.
He thought his house was secure and safe, but found that it just couldn't stand.
A storm blew in with some flooding, too. El Nino, perhaps, of that day?
It shook that house that was on the sand. It lifted and blew it away.
The house the man built on solid rock stood firm in the midst of the storm.
Because he built it secure and safe, the storm couldn't do any harm.
We always build for eternity. Make sure you stand firm every day.
Just plant your feet on the Solid Rock, or Satan might blow you away.

THE TEN VIRGINS

Long, long ago and far away, the bride had no attention.
The groom was honored at the feast, and she was never mentioned.
One groom delayed his pompous stroll. Ten maids were filled with wonder.
They trimmed their lamps and closed their eyes, awaiting him in slumber.
At midnight hour the cry went out, "Here comes the charming bridegroom!
Arise from sleep, relight your lamps, and come into the feast room."
Now, five of them had oil enough, their lamps were trimmed and burning.
The other five had none at all. Their stomachs started churning.
"Please share with us. We have no light," the foolish maidens uttered.
"Go buy your own. We need our oil," the wise ones quickly muttered.
So off the foolish ones did go. Their strides kept getting faster.
When they returned the door was shut!--A terrible disaster!
"Please open up," they cried aloud. "It's time that we extolled you."
"The door is shut," the keeper said. "I'm sorry. I don't know you."
When Christ stands up and says, "It's done, I'll give you what I owe you."
Don't let the Master have to say, "I'm sorry. I don't know you."

THE LOST COIN

A woman lost a precious coin, and she began to panic.
She cleaned her house quite thoroughly, and swept 'til she was frantic.
Of course, she had to light the lamp to find her precious money.
And when the coin was found at last, her countenance was sunny.
She called her friends and neighbors in to join the celebration.
Her coin was lost, but now is found, a joyous situation.
When one lost sinner bows before God's throne with grief and sadness,
The angels nod their heads and smile. Their hearts are filled with gladness.

POWER

Christ met with His disciples before He said goodbye.
"You must stay in Jerusalem, for Power from on high.
I'll send the Holy Spirit My Father promised you.
You'll preach the Word with fervor, and mighty works you'll do.
You need to preach this message in countries far and near.
You'll speak the Word with boldness and do it without fear".
And as they listened to Him, before their very eyes,
He started levitating, and He began to rise.
A cloud then covered Jesus and took Him from their sight.
And while they gazed in wonder, two men appeared in white.
"Why are you gazing upward, and looking for your Friend?
The sky will split asunder, this Christ will come again."
The stunned and dazed disciples went to Jerusalem.
They tarried in an upper room for Power to descend.
With prayers and supplications they unified their souls.
And Peter spoke with passion. Christ's life he did extol.

While waiting for the Spirit to fill their inner space,
They chose a new disciple to take the traitor's place.
Their waiting soon was over. There came a rush of air.
And cloven tongues of fire descended on them there.
New languages were spoken, the Spirit touched each tongue.
They now could reach all people. Their mission had begun.
The people all around them were shocked to hear them speak
In Arabic, Italian, in Spanish and in Greek.
And others mocked and snickered, "They must be filled with wine."
And Peter said it wasn't so, it was the Lord's design.
He boldly stood and told them of Jesus' humble birth,
How He was scorned, rejected, throughout His life on earth.
"You crucified the Son of God and nailed Him to a tree.
The grave could not contain Him. He rose triumphantly.
He went away to heaven and soon will come again
To take His chosen people to live and reign with Him."
And Peter heard some mutter, "We don't know what to do."
He called them to repentance, to live their lives anew.
Some heard the Word with gladness, and on that very day
Three thousand souls were baptized. Their sins were washed away.
These souls, then, spread the message. More people were baptized,
And they did many wonders, as Joel prophesied.

FOOD FROM HEAVEN

Together, John and Peter went up to pray one day.
As they walked to the Temple, a man was in their way.
A crippled man was sitting and begging passers-by.
He could not work for money. On others he relied.
When he saw John and Peter, He said, "I'm hungry sirs.
I cannot make a living. I've been lame since my birth."
Now Peter had compassion, but money was quite scarce.
He offered "food from heaven" in answer to his prayers.
Then Peter looked right at him, as he began to talk.
While offering his right hand, he said, "Rise up and walk."
And right away his ankles, and bones and feet were sound.
He praised the God of heaven with joyous leaps and bounds.
The people looked with wonder. "What happened to this man?"
And Peter gladly told them, "It is the Great I Am.
The One you persecuted and put upon a tree.
Repent and be converted to live eternally."

PETER'S VISION

When Peter climbed the roof top to offer prayers again,
He prayed 'til he was hungry, and would have eaten, then.
But God gave him a vision he did not understand.
A sheet came down from heaven with pigs and rats and clams.
And then, he heard God speaking, "Arise, and kill and eat."
"O no! my Lord," said Peter, "I eat no unclean meat."
Again he heard God speaking. He told him what to do.
"Don't call these creatures common. I've cleansed them all for you."
While Peter stood and wondered about this strange display,
God spoke again the third time, then, whisked the sheet away.
Now Peter was quite baffled. "What did it indicate?"
Three men came by to see him. They stood outside the gate.
The Spirit said, "Now Peter, I'll tell you what to do.
Go down and meet these people. They will enlighten you."
They made the introductions, inquiries were made
As to their little mission. And this is what they said,
"A Gentile named Cornelius, a man of discipline
Received some words from heaven to bid you come to him."
They stayed that night with Peter and lodged there, at his place,
Then, went to Caesarea, to seek Cornelius' face.
Immediately Cornelius fell down at Peter's feet.
"I'm just a man." said Peter, "Stand up. Don't worship me."
The house was filled with Gentiles, to his astonishment.
And right away it struck him just what the vision meant.
"You know it's not the custom for Jews to meet with you.
But God said no one's common, and told me what to do.
"He said all men are equal and precious in His sight.
They all must hear this message, brown, yellow, black and white."
As Peter was expounding the Word of God to them,
The Holy Ghost descended upon those godly men.
They now could preach the message in many languages.
Then Peter said, "Get baptized." And they were truly blessed.

PETER'S ESCAPE

When Herod saw their mighty works, and watched the Christians grow,
He was quite mad, put James to death. It pleased the people so.
He sought out Peter, had him bound, and put him in the jail,
Put sixteen soldiers 'round about, his actions to curtail.
They shackled him to two of them, they wanted him to stay.
But in the night an angel came and took this saint away.
Now Peter must have known his friends had met to say a prayer
In John Mark's home (his mother's house). So Peter went right there.
When Rhoda heard somebody knock she went to let him in.
When she saw Peter standing there, she turned around and ran.
"Hey! Peter's at the door!" she said. "You're crazy!" one man cried.
"O no, I'm not! Please come and see," this little maiden sighed.
And when they opened up the door and saw him standing there,
He told them of his strange ordeal, and how God answered prayer.

DORCAS

A lady lived in Joppa, and Dorcas was her name.
She made clothes for the needy, the sick, the blind, the lame.
So many people loved her for all that she had done.
The garments and the blankets, the coats were all homespun.
One day this godly woman took sick and passed away.
Two men went unto Peter to tell of their dismay.
Now Peter was in Lydda, not far from where they were.
He rose and went to Joppa to see what had occurred.
The widows all were waiting inside the upper room,
Where they had placed the body, awaiting that cold tomb.
O how the widows suffered. They cried and wept and moaned,
Displaying all the garments and coats her hands had sewn.
But Peter said, "Please exit. I need to kneel and pray."
And what a prayer was spoken for Dorcas on that day.
It shook the gates of heaven, and strength came from the Lord.
Then Peter said, "Get up now." Her life had been restored.
The saints and all the widows, then spread the word with glee.
And many souls converted to Christianity.

STEPHEN

The Hebrews and the Grecians were quick to disagree.
The widows were neglected and very much in need.
So seven men were chosen to meet the widows' needs,
To labor for the members, and do the menial deeds.
Contention rose when Stephen worked miracles galore.
The rulers couldn't stand him. His works they did abhor.
They called a courtroom session. He faced a solemn charge
Of blasphemy and treason. The list became quite large.
When asked to give a reason why he should not be tried,
His face looked like an angel, as Christ was glorified.
And Stephen had a vision when offering up a prayer.
He saw the heavens open with Jesus standing there.
The rulers of the Temple were livid as they said,
"Take Stephen from this city and stone him 'til he's dead."
The men took off their garments and left them at Saul's feet.
They gathered rocks around them to do this wicked deed.
And when the stones were hurled, he prayed, "Forgive them, Lord."
And now this mighty warrior awaits his just reward.

THE ROAD TO DAMASCUS

Saul went into the rulers. He thought it quite unfair
That Christians fled the city, and scattered everywhere.
"I'm going to Damascus. I need authority
To round up all the Christians and bring them back with me."
And as he traveled onward, down that Damascus road,
A light came down from heaven, and it was all aglow.
The forcefulness was stunning. It knocked him to his knees.
He heard a voice from heaven, "You're persecuting Me."
"Is that You, Lord, that's speaking?" Saul trembled as he cried.
"Yes, I'm the risen Savior, the One you crucified."
He trembled as he questioned, "What would You have me do?"
"Arise, go to the city. Word will be given you."
When Saul arose he fasted, for he had lost his sight.
His vision was affected by that celestial light.
A man named Ananias was fearful for his life
When God said, "Go and find him and give him back his sight."
"Now, Lord, You know his background. He's tortured folks like me!"
"Just go, and I'll be with you. A changed man you will see."
When Ananias touched him, to give him back his sight,
The scales fell off, and Saul arose and went to be baptized.
And Saul began his mission, went to the Synagogue
To preach the risen Savior, His Name to praise and laud.
The Jews then sought to kill him, but he escaped that night.
His friends planned his departure before the morning light.
For reasons we're not sure of, his name was changed to Paul.
And thus began a journey so great and powerful.

JUPITER AND MERCURY

The Lord said, "I want Barnabas and Paul to work for Me."
So they set sail, and preached the Word each Sabbath, faithfully.
In Lycaonia they found a man lame from his birth.
Of course they healed this crippled man and gave to him self-worth.
The people treated them like gods, with no apology,
For Barnabas was Jupiter, and Paul was Mercury.
The Priest of Jupiter then brought some oxen and some wreathes
To make a simple sacrifice because of their great deeds.
When Paul and Barnabas heard this, they tore their clothes and ran.
"Why are you doing such a thing? Like you, we're only men."
They didn't make that sacrifice. They took Paul out instead,
And threw some heavy stones at him, and left him there for dead.
They dragged him through the city gates, while friends stood all around.
To their amazement Paul came to, and got up off the ground.

MACEDONIA

One day Paul said to Barnabas, "Let's visit once again
The brethren we have taught before, to help and strengthen them."
We'll take John Mark along with us to help," said Barnabas.
"O no, we won't! Not on your life! He chickened out on us.
Remember in Pamphylia, Mark couldn't take the heat?
When things got just a little rough this young man got cold feet."
Contention was quite painful when each man refused to move,
And so the two friends parted, and I'm sure God disapproved.
John Mark and Barnabas set sail for Cyprus' sunny shore,
While Paul and Silas traveled to Cilicia and more.
Paul went to Macedonia, where he had heard the cry
To go and preach the gospel there, and so he did comply.
Because they didn't have a church, each Sabbath they did meet
Outside, upon a river bank, and souls were blessed, indeed.
A young girl in the city there would follow them around.
A demon spirit lived in her. She really was unsound.

Paul told that evil spirit to come out and go away.
The spirit had no other choice. He left that very day.
There were some greedy people who made money from this maid,
And when she lost the demon, it cut off all their trade.
These men were filled with anger now, and did prevaricate.
So Paul and Silas had to go before the magistrate.
The magistrate was told that they caused trouble in the town.
So he commanded that these men beat Paul and Silas down.
They shackled them in prison so they could not get away.
That night old Paul and Silas sang, and they began to pray.
An earthquake shook the prison doors. Each man could then take flight.
The warden, thinking all had fled, wanted to take his life.
But Paul said, "Wait! We all are here. Not one of us is gone."
The keeper of the prison came and fell upon the ground.
"What must I do that I might have eternal life?" he cried.
"Believe on Christ and all your house will then be justified."
This trembling warden took these men and washed their many stripes.
He and his household now believed, and they were all baptized.

MARS HILL

When Paul went into Athens, his heart was grieved within.
Idolatry was rampant among Athenians.
He preached the risen Savior within the Synagogue.
The people were quite troubled with news of this strange God.
So Paul was then invited to speak upon Mars Hill.
Now, this was such an honor, and really quite a thrill.
He said, "Ye men of Athens, to me it is quite plain
That you are superstitious. Now let me please explain.
As I passed by, I noticed an altar up ahead.
I saw this large inscription, 'The Unknown God,' it said.
You ignorantly worship the God you never knew.
He is the One, my brothers, I introduced to you.
He made the world, the heavens, and everything within.
He doesn't dwell in Temples. He isn't made by hands.
He made all nations equal. One blood flows through all men.
We are His sons and daughters. We live and move in Him.
Since we are all His children, we should not think of Him
As just a precious metal engraved by sinful man.
When you did not know better, God overlooked your sin.
But now commands all people to come and worship Him.
One day He's going to judge us for what we've done and said,
By Christ the righteous Savior, whom God raised from the dead."

PAUL'S WORK IN CORINTH

When Paul arrived in Corinth, he found a family there.
Aquila and Priscilla were such a lovely pair.
I'm sure their occupation Paul could appreciate.
Tent making was their business. He, too, made that his trade.
And while he worked in Corinth, and preached each Sabbath Day,
The Jews there, gave him trouble, and wished he'd go away.
"Your blood be on your own heads. You really are unfair.
The Gentiles now will hear me. I've done my duty here."
For eighteen months he taught them, and never did he shrug.
The Jews made insurrection, and brought him to the judge.
He wouldn't even listen, but threw the charges out.
"That's not my jurisdiction. That's not what I'm about."
The Greeks then grabbed the ruler of that great Synagogue,
And he was brought to judgment, was beaten and was flogged.
Paul went around the country, and reasoned with the Jews,
Proclaiming Christ the Savior, preaching the Gospel News.

PAUL'S YEARS IN EPHESUS

Paul spent two years in Ephesus, and preached the message there,
Baptizing those who heard the Word. Christ's love he did declare.
He worked so many miracles, cast out some devils, too.
The place was steeped in devilry, but souls were born anew.
They burned their books on the occult, much to some folks' dismay.
More than a million dollars worth went up in smoke that day.
Demetrius, a silversmith, made silver shrines to sell,
In honor of Diana whom the people loved so well.
When Paul began to preach the Word, and baptized many souls,
Demetrius lost plenty of his silver and his gold.
He called the other silversmiths to see what could be done.
"Diana's great!" they cried aloud. "We'll have to bring him down."
When all of Ephesus heard this, confusion came about.
"Diana's great! Diana's great!" Two hours they did shout.
At last the town clerk took control, "These men did not defraud.
Bring them before a civil court and do things by the law."
At last the people settled down, no riots, no hoop-lah.
Paul hugged the members, then, set sail for Macedonia.

PAUL'S LENGTHY SERMON

Paul sailed away from Phillipi, and Troas came in sight.
And after staying seven days he preached 'til way past night.
A certain man named Eutychus sat on the window sill.
Long sermons made him drowsy and I guess he had his fill.
His head began to nod and droop, his nerves were set on edge.
At last his body did succumb, and he fell off the ledge.
He fell three stories down below. I'm sure he hit his head.
When they went down to get this man, they thought that he was dead.
Paul had to stop his preaching, then, to save this young man's life.
I guess he gave him CPR. That young man did survive.
Paul must have had a lot to say, his sermon he resumed
After they ate, when morning came, at last they left the room.

DANGER IN JERUSALEM

When Paul went to Jerusalem, his life was all but dull.
The elders told him people said he preached against the law.
"Soon they will know that you are here, and put this charge on you.
You need to purify yourself to show this isn't true."
So Paul took four men with him to the Temple the next day,
Was purified, to let them know the law he did obey.
And when the Jews from Asia saw Paul in the Temple there,
They stirred up all the multitude. His treatment was unfair.
They said the Sanctuary was polluted with the Greeks,
That Paul taught people everywhere the law they need not keep.
They took poor Paul and dragged him from the Synagogue that day,
They meant to kill him on the spot--get him out of their way.
But word got out, Jerusalem was going to kill this man.
They had to send the National Guard to make these folks disband.
The Captain of the National Guard said, "Put his legs in chains."
He asked the people what he'd done to make them so insane.
The people then were all confused, not knowing what to say,
And so the Captain of the Guard said, "Take this man away."
They led him to the Castle where Paul said, "May I now speak?"
The Captain of the National Guard said, "Man, can you speak Greek?"
And with permission given, Paul spoke in the Hebrew tongue.
He told of his conversion and the wrong that he had done.
They listened 'til they had enough, then, said, "Away with him!"
The Captain then led Paul away and had him bound again.
He said, "Take Paul and clobber him to satisfy the claim."
"You cannot beat a Roman, Sir," the man heard Paul exclaim.
They had to take the shackles off for fear they'd lose their lives,
If they should beat him half to death, when they weren't authorized.
Again Paul went to Council for the priests to check him out.
The High Priest, Ananias, said to slap him in the mouth.

DANGER IN JERUSALEM (cont.)

But Paul said "O you washed out wall. My God will slap you, too!"
The people standing 'round about were wondering what to do.
Now half of them were Pharisees in that assembly's throng.
The other half were Sadducees. They did not get along.
Then Paul decided he would play some mind games, so he cried,
"Hey! I'm a Pharisee, and I believe the dead will rise."
The Sadducees were livid. "We do not believe that way."
A fight broke out among them, and court adjourned that day.
They turned on Paul and surely would have tried to do him in,
But then the Captain of the Guard sent men to rescue him.
And in the morning forty Jews vowed not to drink or eat
Until they killed this reprobate. They tried to be discreet.
"We'd like to talk to him again," they told the soldiers' Chief,
While planning to assassinate and make him obsolete.
Paul's nephew told the Captain all about this plot that day.
Almost five hundred soldiers then, escorted him away.
Paul had to go to Felix' court, who trembled at his word.
Then Festus heard the charges, but the Jews he reassured.
Agrippa said he'd like to hear what Paul would have to say.
He almost made a convert of this mighty king that day.
Then Paul appealed to Caesar, since he was a Roman Jew.
They boarded him upon a ship, and bade him fond adieu.
Paul's nephew told the Captain all about this plot that day.
Almost five hundred soldiers then, escorted him away.
Paul had to go to Felix' court, who trembled at his word.
Then Festus heard the charges, but the Jews he reassured.
Agrippa said he'd like to hear what Paul would have to say.
He almost made a convert of this mighty king that day.
Then Paul appealed to Caesar, since he was a Roman Jew.
They boarded him upon a ship, and bade him fond adieu.

SHIPWRECKED

The ship on which Paul traveled came into a port one day.
The warden of Augustus' band told Paul to slip away.
He knew Paul's clothes were dirty and he needed personal care.
Assured that Paul would soon return, he let him venture there.
And when they sailed to Myra he was transferred to a boat
That soon set sail for Italy for his new episode.
They soon passed by Salmone where another port was found.
A lot of time was spent there, when the crew just hung around.
At last when it was time to sail, Paul had to tell those men
That sailing was too dangerous, and harm would come to them.
But they believed the master and the owner of the ship,
Who told them that the boat was sound, and very well-equipped.
But soon, the winter storms would come and blow the ship away.
They set sail for Phenice, a safe place for them to stay.
Their purpose was to go ashore when they sailed close to Crete,
But when a hurricane arose they drifted back to sea.
The ship was being tossed about and they were at death's door.
They picked a lot of cargo up and tossed it overboard.
And when they thought their time was up, and they would all be dead,
Paul stood up in the midst of them, and this is what he said,
"You should have listened to me when I told you not to go.
You brought this harm upon yourselves. You know I told you so.
An angel of the Lord came down, and said, 'Don't be afraid.
I'll spare the lives of all on board,' is what the angel said."
And after they had tossed about for fourteen days and nights,
The crew aboard were positive that land was in their sight.
Again, Paul seemed to take command. "You need to eat," he said.
"You need to get some nourishment, or you might all be dead."
He blessed the food, then, passed it out, and everyone did eat.
The ship was still too heavy, so they cast out half the wheat.
And when they tried to get to shore, they ran the ship aground.
The back was broken by the waves, the front was stuck, they found.
The soldiers thought the men on board would swim and get away.
They said, "Let's kill these prisoners before we have to pay."
But then the kind Centurion who wanted to save Paul,
Said, "Swim to shore or grab some wood. Hope for a miracle."
All made it safely to the land. Not one of them was dead.
The God of all the Universe preserved them, as Paul said.

MELITA

The people on that island were kind as they could be.
They made a fire to warm them, for it was cold, you see.
When Paul had gathered kindling, a viper bit his hand.
It stayed there clinging to him. The natives watched it hang.
Paul shook that brutal viper into the coals of fire,
And in the natives' thinking, a god had just transpired.
The chief man on the island, then, opened up his home.
Three days they spent in comfort, Paul and his chaperone.
The father of this Chieftain was sick and almost died.
His blood was oozing from him. His pain would not subside.
Paul put his hands upon him, and then began to pray,
And soon the fever left him, and strength came back that day.
When all the natives heard this, they brought their sick to Paul.
Led by the Holy Spirit, he healed them, one and all.
Since Paul appealed to Caesar, he had to get to Rome.
The natives gave provisions. They left their island home.
They reached their destination, were given to the guards.
Paul and his soldier escort were in a separate ward.
He called the Jews together, informed them of his case.
Then, preached God's Holy Kingdom and Christ's amazing grace.
For two years Paul was preaching of God's eternal love.
His labors were recorded in heaven's book above.

AB ASPECT Books

We invite you to view the complete
selection of titles we publish at:
www.ASPECTBooks.com

We encourage you to write us
with your thoughts about this,
or any other book we publish at:
info@ASPECTBooks.com

ASPECT Books' titles may be purchased in
bulk quantities for educational, fund-raising,
business, or promotional use.
bulksales@ASPECTBooks.com

Finally, if you are interested in seeing your
own book in print, please contact us at:
publishing@ASPECTBooks.com

We are happy to review your manuscript at no charge.

www.ingramcontent.com/pod-product-compliance
Lightning Source LLC
Chambersburg PA
CBHW070546170426
43200CB00011B/2573